LET
THERE BE

Faith Over Fear

Volume I

By Aldrika Boyle

Edited, Formatted & Published by

Wade Christian Publishing LLC

www.wadepublishers.com

info@wadepublishers.com

Let There Be Life: Faith Over Fear Vol: I

Written by Aldrika Boyle

Cover Design by Aria Jones

Paperback ISBN: 979-8-9857363-6-6

E-Book ISBN: 979-8-9857363-7-3

Dedication

This book is dedicated to my husband Barrion and our three children Gabrielle, Barrion Jr., and Madison.

Faith has held us together.

Table of Contents

Faith Over Fear

On January 23, 1995, the doctor's report read: a black female, 26 years old, with multiple cysts, tumors, and infection, must have a hysterectomy. That was one of the scariest days of my life. The desire to become a mother seemed unlikely and became lost in my heart. I was so sick I couldn't walk, and the doctor said I needed a complete hysterectomy; that was the only answer.

The Beginning

Three years earlier, I got married on April 18, 1992. I was 23 years old and full of life with many dreams. One thing I wanted more than anything was to be a mom. I loved children, and becoming a mom was my heart's desire.

I never thought it would be a problem for me to get pregnant, so I stayed on birth control the first year we were married. However, in the second year of our marriage, I stopped taking birth control because we truly wanted a child. It never dawned on me we were going to be up for a Spiritual Battle.

After a year of being off birth control, I had difficulty conceiving. I became concerned and went to the doctor to see why. To get pregnant, we took various tests and fertility drugs. Everything we tried didn't work. Nevertheless, as months went on, we never gave up. We stopped using fertility drugs and continually tried to conceive.

During this time, I shared with my Bible study group and prayer partners that I was standing in faith, trusting, and believing in God for a baby. My faith did waver sometimes, and I became discouraged. Each time I took a pregnancy test, it came back negative. I would ask myself, "What is wrong with me?" or, I would ask God, "Where I was missing it?" I was saved, lived a righteous life, and spread God's Word to others. I didn't understand why I couldn't get pregnant.

Hence, I began to search God's Word and look up women in the Bible who had trouble having children to see what they did as a guide. At this point, I realized I was walking in faith one minute and then walking in fear the next minute. I recognized that God does not move on emotions. God moves by faith only.

As time went by, I decided to do what I knew best. I had to build up my spirit man on the inside of me and stand in faith only. I had to look at only what God's Word said and not look at what my situation was saying. I began to go on a mission to find scriptures that lined up with what I believed God for:

Psalms 113:9 (KJV) He makes the barren woman abide in the house as a joyful mother of children.

Isaiah 54:1 (KJV) Shout for joy, O barren one, you have borne no child; Break forth into joyful shouting and cry aloud.

These were the first two scriptures I started confessing every day. Every morning I woke up, I would confess God's Word over my life. I boldly spoke the scriptures so much until I made it personal. I would put my name in each verse and say:

Psalms 113:9 (KJV) The Father God makes Aldrika abide in the house as a joyful mother of children. I said it in the morning, during the day, and at night before bed. I would get so excited! I would also confess this scripture, **Isaiah 54:1 (KJV) Shout for joy, Aldrika, O barren one, you have not borne no child; Break forth into joyful shouting and cry aloud.**

Father God was saying to me **"shout for joy!"** As I shouted for joy, the other scripture that came to my heart was **Psalms 126:5 (KJV) They that sow in tears shall reap in Joy**. Then the Holy Spirit on the inside of me said, make it personal, put your name in the verse. Then I spoke aloud with all my heart, **"What *Aldrika* sow in tears, I will reap in joy."** Father God was letting me know that His Holy Word is true! As I confessed the Word of God, my faith grew stronger and stronger, and my fears became weaker and weaker. Nevertheless, I was still getting negative pregnancy tests, and time went on. Every time fear and hopelessness tried to sneak in, God's promises became "Rhema" light to me. God's promises began to become more real to me each day. I believed God, and built my faith muscles by confessing the Word of God. I put faith scriptures in my heart, and my relationship with God grew stronger and stronger each day. I would confess **Psalm 138:8 (KJV) The Lord will make perfect those things that concern me.** Then I would say, **The Lord will make perfect those things that concern _Aldrika._** Placing your name in the scriptures makes the scriptures personal. You are letting God know you believe in His Word, and you know it will come to pass for you.

Proverbs 3:5-6 (KJV) says Trust in the Lord with all your heart; and lean not unto your own understanding. In all your ways acknowledge Him, and He will direct your path.

The keyword to this scripture is "trust." I had to say, "**_Aldrika_**, trust in the Lord with all your heart and do not lean on your own understanding, but in all your ways acknowledge the Father God, and he will direct your path. When you are standing in faith and believing in God, you must trust God no matter what. As a believer, you must trust God no matter how bad you hurt. You must trust God no matter how much you cry. You must trust God, no matter how terrible your situation is. Your trust in God is the only way you will overcome all adversities.

Hence, I didn't care what it looked like. Each month the pregnancy test came back negative. I sowed many tears. As each tear fell, I would pull myself together and say with trust and belief in my heart, "Aldrika, what you sow in tears, you will reap in joy!"; because that is what the Word of God says. Then I would say, **"Be it unto me according to Your Word."** These are the words Mary said when the angel of the Lord told her she would be with a child. She had not been with a man, but she trusted God and obeyed His Word, and our Savior Jesus was born unto Mary. **Luke 1:38 (KJV)**

The next thing I did was act like the blessing had already come to pass. I bought a little boy and little girl outfit and a maternity shirt. I put it in the baby room as I walked in faith. Walking in faith means you must act as if it has already happened.

2 Corinthians 4:18 (KJV) tells us that While we look not at the things which are seen, but at the things which are not seen, for the things that are seen are temporary, but the things that are not seen are eternal.

What I was seeing was a negative pregnancy test. I could have accepted it, or believed what others were saying: "Maybe you just can't have any children". However, I chose to believe the Word of God. I spoke, "Let there be LIFE in this situation." I knew my womb was not dead but alive.

Faith Muscles Growing

Isaiah 55:8 – 13 (KJV) tells us For my thoughts are not your thoughts, neither are your ways my ways, says the Lord. For as the heavens are higher than the earth, so are my ways higher than your ways, and my thoughts than your thoughts. As the rain and snow fall to the earth, and water the earth, and do not return up, but water the earth, and bring forth a bud, so shall the Father God Word be that goes forth out of "your" mouth, it will not return void, but it will accomplish that which you send it.

This scripture is saying to you that you must pray the Word of God. God wants you to pray His Word, for as you pray the Word of God, your prayer will come to pass. It will not fall on deaf ears; it will come to pass because that is what the Father God is saying in His Word. God was telling me, "Aldrika, pray my Word. Do not pray how you feel, do not pray what you see, but pray the Word of God. Father God is saying His Word will not return unto Him void. God is compassionate, and He loves us. We, as parents, tell our children that they must follow instructions. The same rule applies to adults. We must obey God's instructions and pray the Word of God.

Romans 10:17 (KJV) So then faith comes by hearing, and hearing the Word of God. This verse tells us that we cannot have microwave faith. We cannot put a time limit on God. God knows the right moment to bless us. For example, have you ever planted a seed in the ground, woke up the next day, and the flower bloomed? No, that is not how it works. First, the seed is planted. Next, you water and feed the seed. Then, you wait for the harvest. Seed, time, then harvest. We may get weary when standing in faith because some prayers take longer to get answered than others. But the Word of God says in **Galatians 6:9 (KJV) Let us not be weary in well doing: for in due season, we shall reap, if we faint not.** During the waiting time is when we water and feed the seed. We water and feed the seed with praise and worship, and confess the Word of God over the situation. This is how faith works. Confess the scriptures, and make them personal by putting your name in them. Praise and worship God because He inhabits the praises of His people. Sow seeds into others' lives and help someone else reach their goal. As you do these things, God is working it out for you.

Hebrews 11:6 (KJV) But without faith it is impossible to please God: for he is a rewarder of them that diligently seek him. You can pray this scripture in the following way: (Father God, as I stand in faith, I'm grateful and aim to please you. I thank you for rewarding me as I diligently seek you. In Jesus' Name, I pray. Amen).

As you are standing in faith you must trust and believe God will move on your behalf. Pray the scripture and not how you feel.

I Peter 5:6 tells us that we must humble ourselves under the mighty hands of God, that He may exalt you in due time. As we humble ourselves, our faith, trust, and belief grow on the inside of us. Try praying this scripture for example: (Father God, I believe your Word is true, so I humble myself unto You, for You will exalt me in due time.)

The TEST

On January 23, 1995, early that morning, I woke up, and was in so much pain I couldn't walk. I was cramping so badly that my husband had to take me to the emergency room. The doctor examined me and stated that I needed to have a hysterectomy. I had so many cysts and tumors that they couldn't count them. I was also full of infection. The doctor said we needed to have surgery that day, but in my heart and spirit, I knew that was not what I had been praying and believing God for. So, I asked the doctor whether there were any more options. The doctor said, "I can give you an antibiotic to clear the infection, and in five days, we will have to reexamine you to schedule surgery." With tears rolling down my face, I told the doctor and the nurse, "You can schedule the surgery, but I promise you, when you examine me in the next five days, my body will be healed, and it will be healed Supernaturally." The doctor looked at me and said, "I hope so." My husband rolled me out in the wheelchair. I got in the car and said to myself, "It is time for a spiritual battle." I had two choices; I could have just given up on my desire to become a mom, or I could stand in faith and believe God for my healing. The easy way out was to give in, but I was not going to give in because I knew God's Word, and I believed God at His Word.

Now it was time to do all I knew to do. I knew what I had been praying for, and in my heart, I knew I was going to receive my heart's desire. God told me to pray His Word, so I pulled out God's promises that were deep in my heart. I knew what God's Word said, and this time, my faith was stronger than ever before. So, I began praying: "Father God, in the name of Jesus, You said in Your Word in **Psalms 37: 4-5 (KJV) Delight thyself in the Lord, and He will give thee, Aldrika, the desires of my heart**. (You can insert your name and pray this prayer also.) As far as I was concerned, this sickness was a mountain, and it had to be moved. So, I started to pray Mark 11:23-25.

Mark 11:23 (KJV) For verily I say unto you, that whosoever shall say unto this mountain, be thou removed, and be cast into the sea, and shall not doubt in his heart, but shall believe that those things which he saith shall come to pass; he shall have whatsoever he saith.

Mark 11:24 (KJV)Therefore, I say unto you (*Aldrika*), **(***Put your name here***) believe that you receive, and you shall have what you say.**

Nevertheless, the most essential part of these three scriptures is in the next verse, **Mark 11:25**. When you (*Aldrika*) *(Put your name here*) **stand praying, forgive, if ye have any unforgiveness in your heart, you must forgive so God can forgive you. Blessings come with forgiveness in your heart.**

I'm telling you, I did it all! I began to praise and worship God with all my heart. I prayed the Word of God, confessed the promises of God, and was anointed with oil. As believers, we must understand that the Holy Spirit is in us, and God wants us to trust Him in all things. The pain at this moment was heavy, and the tears of my future rolled down my face. I was like the woman with the issue of blood. I knew that one touch from God would change this situation around. I also knew that with every tear I sowed, I would reap it in joy, because that is what God's Word says in **Psalms126:5 (KJV).** I just had to keep believing.

Nevertheless, I had different people come to check on me, and I knew it was only out of love because they were worried about me. Some people said, "Maybe you just cannot have children" or, "Don't put your life on the line trying to get pregnant." Many more doubtful and unbelievable comments were stated. Respectfully, I told everyone that I believed God, and knew what the Word of God said.

One of my prayer partners came to work looking for me; she didn't know I was out sick. She had just come from a mid-week Prayer Service. The Pastor stood up with a bottle of anointed oil and said, "The Holy Spirit told him that the bottle of anointed oil would be used to anoint a lady's ovaries that week. She stood up and got the anointed oil because she knew I was standing in faith, believing God to have a baby. She didn't know at that time I had become sick, but God knew. Father God will bless you through whoever He has to, for the blessing to get to you.

Hence, she received the bottle of anointed oil for me. Upon her arrival at my office, she found out I was at home sick. In the meantime, I was home praying the Word of God, confessing the Word of God, and having praise and worship. When she arrived at my home, the presence of the Lord was in the atmosphere. "The Battle is not Yours, it's the Lord's" song was playing and she knocked on the door. She walked into my home with the divine power of

14

the Lord Jesus Christ! God used her to pray over my husband and me. She rubbed both of us with the Holy anointed oil. We boldly praised God for His healing power! We knew God would heal me.

Suddenly, and I mean suddenly, God moved! The pain was gone. I could walk (when I couldn't walk moments before). I started to jump and run around the table as the power of God flowed through my body. I felt God's Super-Natural power flowing in me! Tears of joy started flowing down my face as I knew I was healed.

My healing happened on a Wednesday. The following day, I was scheduled to be reexamined for surgery. The doctor did the test, and they realized the cysts and the tumors were gone! Two months later, I was pregnant without using fertility drugs.

Moreover, the pregnancy was without morning sickness and no-weight gain. Throughout my pregnancy, I called the baby "Anointed." I spoke life to my baby and believed God for a healthy baby. We didn't find out what the sex of the baby was, we just wanted a healthy baby.

Nevertheless, this was an exciting time for all my family and friends as they saw God moving Supernaturally in our lives. Our baby shower was large. Friends and family brought many gifts. Our "Anointed" baby was blessed from the very beginning.

The Birth

The time had come for our new baby to enter the world. The doctors decided we needed to induce the labor. It was forty-one weeks, and the baby still had not arrived. We were admitted into the hospital at 5:30 am on January 22, 1996. The doctor said the baby should be born within the next few hours. Again, God was in motion to show up and show out. Labor went on for twenty-two hours, and at 4:59 am on January 23, 1996, **Gabrielle Shalom Boyle** entered this world. She was 5 pounds 11 ounces. She was healthy and full of life.

We named her Gabrielle, which means GOD is my strength, and Shalom, which means Jehovah is peace.

In conclusion, it was January 23, 1995, when I was attacked by the enemy and was told that I needed to have a hysterectomy. I could have cried and asked, "Why me?" Instead, I stood firm in faith and believed God. I chose to believe God at His Word. Because of my faith in God's Word, Gabrielle Shalom Boyle was born on January 23, 1996, on the anniversary of the day when the doctors said I needed to have a hysterectomy!

To the person reading this today, no matter what your situation is, everyone goes through night seasons of difficulty. It is what you do in the midst of the dead dark season that matters. Are you going to give up, cave in, quit, or choose life? Life and death are in the power of the tongue. Confessing and believing the Word of God will change any situation around.

If you take the Word of God and apply it to your life, God will move on your behalf. The key is that you must **believe God can, and He will answer your prayers!**

Have Faith, Trust, and Believe.

ABOUT THE AUTHOR

Aldrika Boyle was born in 1968 to Albert and Brenda Butler. She is a native of Baton Rouge, Louisiana. She married Barrion Boyle in 1992 and they have three beautiful children, Gabrielle, Barrion Jr., and Madison Boyle.

Aldrika has two master's degrees. She obtained a Master of Science in Human Resources, and a Master of Science in Management. She also has a Bachelor of Science in Human Services. Aldrika has been in a Leadership role in Human Resources Management for over fifteen years.

Aldrika resides in the Atlanta Metro area where she's a member of Word of Faith Cathedral and has led Discipleship Groups for many years. She is also a Mentor with the Rare Pearls mentoring program of Douglasville, Ga.

Aldrika gave her life to God at an early age. Throughout life's trials and tests, she has learned the true principles of God's Word. Aldrika has learned through faith and believing God's Word that nothing is impossible if you truly believe.

You will see by reading this book how God made the impossible, possible.

Let There be Life!!!

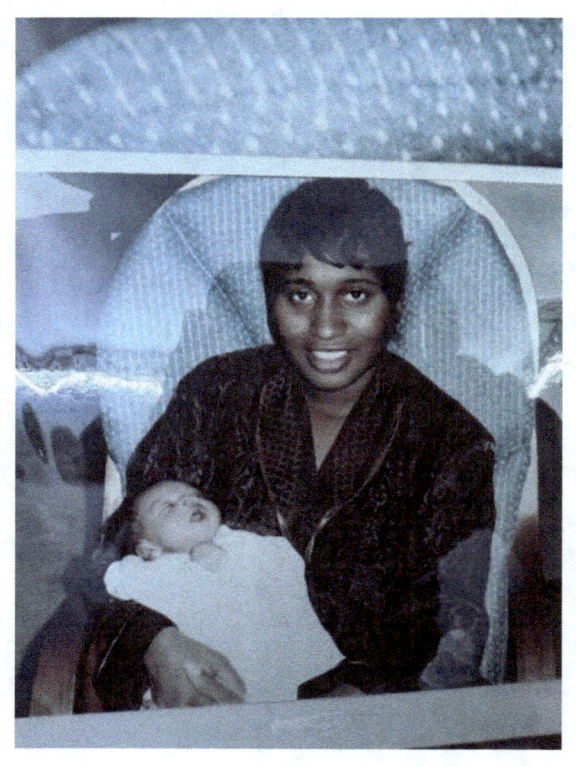

Aldrika Boyle and baby Gabrielle

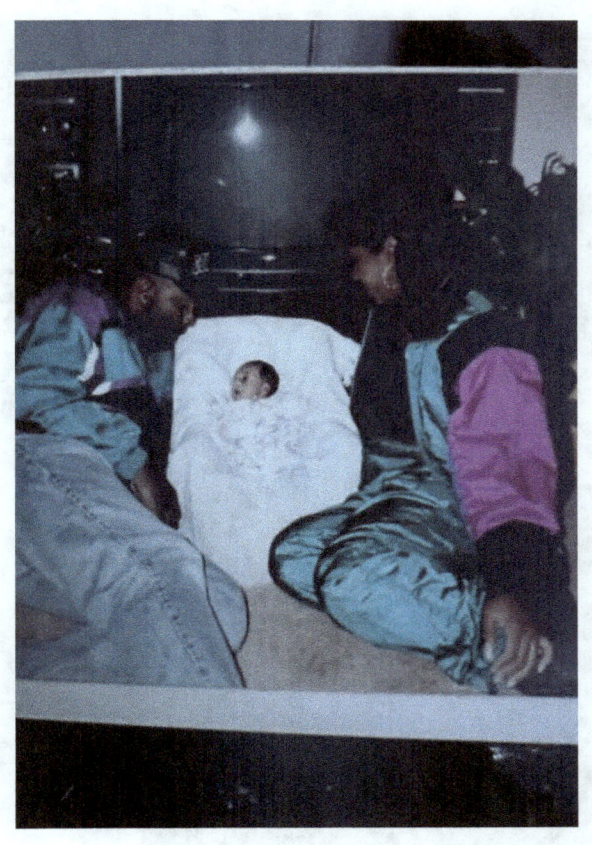

Barrion and Aldrika with baby Gabrielle

**Gabrielle Shalom Boyle's graduation
from college
Bachelor of Science in Accounting 2018**

Aldrika Boyle is the author of the **Faith Over Fear** Book Series. Her first book title is **Let There Be Life: Faith Over Fear Volume I**. Her forthcoming book title is **Death Could Not Hold Me: Faith Over Fear Volume II**.

www.ingramcontent.com/pod-product-compliance
Lightning Source LLC
Chambersburg PA
CBHW060359130626
46553CB00003B/1302